'Because of his baldness and hairiness, he announced that it was a capital offence for anyone either to look down on him as he passed or to mention goats in any context.'

GAIUS SUETONIUS TRANQUILLUS
Born *c.* 70 CE
Died *c.* 130 CE

Taken from Robert Graves's translation of
The Twelve Caesars, first published in 1957.

SUETONIUS IN PENGUIN CLASSICS
The Twelve Caesars

SUETONIUS

Caligula

Translated by
Robert Graves

PENGUIN BOOKS

PENGUIN CLASSICS

UK | USA | Canada | Ireland | Australia
India | New Zealand | South Africa

Penguin Books is part of the Penguin Random House group of companies
whose addresses can be found at global.penguinrandomhouse.com.

This edition published in Penguin Classics 2015
004

Translation copyright © Robert Graves, 1957

The moral right of the translator has been asserted

Set in 10/14.5 pt Baskerville 10 Pro
Typeset by Jouve (UK), Milton Keynes
Printed in Great Britain by Clays Ltd, St Ives plc

A CIP catalogue record for this book is available from the British Library

ISBN: 978–0–141–39792–4

www.greenpenguin.co.uk

MIX
Paper from
responsible sources
FSC® C018179

Penguin Random House is committed to a
sustainable future for our business, our readers
and our planet. This book is made from Forest
Stewardship Council® certified paper.

Gaius Caligula

Germanicus, father of Gaius Caesar, was the son of Drusus and Antonia the younger, and was eventually adopted by Tiberius, his paternal uncle. He served as quaestor five years before he was legally eligible and became consul without holding any of the intermediary offices, and was then appointed to the command of the forces in Germany. When Augustus' death became known, the legions there were unanimously opposed to Tiberius' succession and would have acclaimed Germanicus emperor, but he showed a remarkable example of filial respect and personal integrity by diverting their attention from this project; he took the offensive in Germany, and won a triumph. As consul for the second time he was hurried to the east, where conditions were unsettled, before being able to take office. There he defeated the king of Armenia and reduced Cappadocia to provincial status, but he succumbed to a protracted illness at Antioch, being only thirty-four years old when he died. Because of the dark stains which covered his body and the foam on his lips, poison was suspected; significantly, they also found the heart intact among the ashes after cremation – a heart steeped in poison is supposedly proof against fire.

If we may accept the common verdict, Tiberius craftily arranged Germanicus' death with the advice and assistance of Gnaeus Piso. Piso had been appointed to govern Syria at about the same time, and there, deciding that he must make an enemy either of Germanicus or of Tiberius, took every opportunity to provoke Germanicus, even when on his sickbed, by the meanest acts and speeches – behaviour for which the Senate condemned him to death on his return to Rome, after he had narrowly escaped a popular lynching.

Germanicus is everywhere described as having been of outstanding physical and moral excellence. He was handsome, courageous, a past master of Greek and Latin oratory and learning, conspicuously kind-hearted, and gifted with the ability of winning

universal respect and affection. Only his legs were
somewhat undeveloped, but he strengthened them
by assiduous exercise on horseback after meals. He
often fought and killed an enemy in hand-to-hand
combat, and did not cease to plead cases in the law
courts even when he had gained a triumph. Some of
his Greek comedies are extant, besides other literary
works. At home or abroad he always behaved modestly, would dispense with lictors when visiting any
free or allied town, and offered sacrifices at whatever
tombs of famous men he came across. On deciding
to bury under one mound all the scattered bones of
Varus' fallen legionaries, he led the search party himself and took an active part in the collection. Towards
his detractors Germanicus showed such tolerance
and leniency, regardless of their identity or motives,
that he would not even break with Piso (who was
cancelling his orders and plaguing his subordinates)
until he found that spells and potions were being used
against him. And then he did no more than renounce
his friendship in the traditional manner, and leave tes-
tamentary instructions for his family to take vengeance
on Piso if anything should happen to himself.

Such virtuous conduct brought Germanicus rich

rewards. He was so deeply respected and loved by all his acquaintances that Augustus – I need hardly mention his other relatives – wondered for a long time whether to make him his successor, but at last ordered Tiberius to adopt him. Germanicus, the records show, had won such intense popular devotion that he was in danger of being mobbed to death whenever he arrived at a place or took his leave again. Indeed, when he came back from Germany after suppressing the native uprising, all the praetorian cohorts marched out in welcome, despite orders that only two were to do so, and the entire people of Rome – all ages and ranks and both sexes – flocked as far as the twentieth milestone to meet him.

But the most spectacular proof of the devotion in which Germanicus had been held appeared on the day of his death and immediately afterwards. The populace stoned temples and upset altars; heads of families threw their household gods into the street and abandoned their newly born children. Even the barbarians who were fighting us or one another are said to have made immediate peace as though a domestic tragedy had afflicted the whole world, some princes shaving their own beards and their wives' heads in token of profound grief. The King of Kings himself cancelled his hunting parties and banquets, which is a sign of public mourning in Parthia.

While Rome was still stunned by the first news of his illness and waiting for further bulletins, a rumour that he had recovered went the rounds one evening after dark and sent people rushing to the Capitol with torches and sacrificial victims; so eager were they to fulfil their vows that the temple gates were almost torn down. Tiberius was awakened by the joyful chant:

> All is well again at Rome,
> All is well again at home,
> Here's an end to all our pain:
> Germanicus is well again!

When the news of his death finally broke, neither edicts nor official expressions of sympathy could console the people; mourning continued throughout the festival days of December. The bitterness of their loss was aggravated by the horrors which followed, for everyone believed, and with good reason, that moral respect for Germanicus had alone kept Tiberius from displaying the cruelty of his wicked heart.

5

Germanicus married Agrippina, daughter of Marcus Agrippa and Julia, who bore him nine children. Two died in infancy, and a third, an extremely likeable boy, during early childhood. Livia dedicated a statue of him, dressed as Cupid, to Venus Capitolina; Augustus kept a replica in his bedroom, and used to kiss it fondly whenever he entered. The other children – three girls, Agrippina, Drusilla and Livilla, born in successive years, and three boys, Nero, Drusus and Gaius Caesar – survived their father; but Tiberius later brought charges against Nero and Drusus, whom he persuaded the Senate to execute as public enemies.

Gaius Caesar was born on 31 August, during the consulship shared by his father with Gaius Fonteius Capito. His birthplace is disputed. According to Gnaeus Lentulus Gaetulicus he was born at Tibur, but according to Pliny the Elder at the village of Ambitarvium in the territory of the Treveri, just above Confluens; Pliny supports his view by mentioning certain local altars inscribed 'In Honour of Agrippina's *Puerperium*'. A verse which went the rounds at his accession also suggests that he was born in the winter quarters of the legions:

> Born in a barracks,
>> Reared in the arts of war:
> A noble nativity
>> For a Roman emperor!

The public records, however, give his birthplace as Antium, and my researches convince me that this is correct. Pliny shows that Gaetulicus tried to flatter the proud young *princeps* by pretending that he came from Tibur, a city sacred to Hercules, and that he lied with greater confidence because Germanicus did have a son named Gaius Caesar born there the year before, whose sadly premature death I have already mentioned. Nevertheless, Pliny is himself mistaken, since Augustus' biographers agree that Germanicus' first visit to Gaul took place after he had been consul, by which time Gaius was already born. Moreover, the inscriptions on the altars do not prove Pliny's point, since Agrippina bore Germanicus two daughters in Gaul, and any confinement is a *puerperium*, regardless of the child's sex – girls were then still called *puerae* as often as *puellae*, and boys *puelli* as often as *pueri*. Finally, I have found a letter which Augustus wrote to his granddaughter Agrippina a few months before he died; the Gaius mentioned in it must have been this one, because no other child of that name was alive at the time. It reads, 'Yesterday, I made arrangements for Talarius and Asillius to bring your son Gaius to you on the eighteenth of May, if the gods will. I am also sending with him one of my slaves, a doctor who, as I have told Germanicus in a letter, need not be returned to me if he proves of use to you. Goodbye, my dear Agrippina! Keep well on the way back to your Germanicus.' Clearly, Gaius could not have been born in a country to which he was first taken from Rome at the age of nearly two. These details also weaken my confidence in that anonymous verse about his birth in a barracks. So we are, I think, reduced to accepting the only other authority, namely the public records, especially since Gaius preferred Antium to any other city and treated it as his native place; he even planned, they say, to transfer the seat of imperial government there when he wearied of Rome.

He won his cognomen Caligula from an army joke, because he grew up among the troops and wore the miniature uniform of a private soldier. An undeniable proof of the hold on their affections which this early experience of camp life gave him is that when they rioted at the news of Augustus' death and were ready for any madness, the mere sight of little Gaius calmed them down. As soon as they realized that he was being removed to a neighbouring city to protect him from their violence, they were overcome by contrition; some of them seized and stopped his carriage, pleading to be spared this disgrace.

Gaius also accompanied Germanicus to Syria. On his return he lived with his mother, and next, after she had been exiled, with his great-grandmother Livia Augusta, whose funeral oration he delivered from the Rostra though he had not yet come of age. He then lived with his grandmother Antonia until Tiberius summoned him to Capreae at the age of nineteen. He assumed the adult toga and shaved his first beard on one and the same day, but this was a most informal occasion compared with his brothers' coming-of-age celebrations. The courtiers tried every trick to force him into making complaints against Tiberius – always, however, without success. He not only failed to show any interest in the murder of his relatives, but affected an amazing indifference to his own ill treatment, behaving so obsequiously

to his adoptive grandfather and to the entire household that someone said of him, very neatly, 'Never
was there a better slave, or a worse master.'

Yet even in those days he could not control his
natural brutality. He loved watching tortures and
executions, and, disguised in a wig and a long robe,
abandoned himself nightly to the pleasures of feast-
ing and scandalous living. Tiberius was ready enough
to indulge a passion which Gaius had for theatrical
dancing and singing, on the ground that it might
have a civilizing influence on him. With characteristic
shrewdness, the old emperor had exactly gauged the
young man's vicious inclinations, and would often
remark that Gaius' advent portended his own death
and the ruin of everyone else. 'I am nursing a viper
in Rome's bosom,' he once said; 'I am educating a
Phaethon for the whole world.'

Gaius shortly thereafter married Junia Claudilla,
daughter of the distinguished senator Marcus Silanus.
Then he was appointed augur in place of his brother
Drusus, but transferred to the pontificate before his
inauguration in compliment to his dutiful behaviour
and exemplary life. This encouraged him in the hope
of becoming Tiberius' successor, because Sejanus'

downfall had reduced the court to a shadow of its former self; and when Junia died in childbirth he seduced Ennia, wife of Naevius Macro, the praetorian prefect, not only swearing to marry her if he became emperor, but putting the oath in writing. After Ennia helped him win Macro's support, he assailed Tiberius with poison, as some people think; he issued orders for his ring to be removed while he was still breathing, and when he would not let it go he had him smothered with a pillow. According to one account he throttled Tiberius with his own hands, and when a freedman cried out in protest at this wicked deed he crucified him at once. All this may be true; some writers report that Gaius later confessed to intended if not actual parricide. He would often boast, that is to say, of having carried a dagger into Tiberius' bedroom with the virtuous intention of avenging his mother and brothers; but, according to his own account, he found Tiberius asleep and, restrained by feelings of pity, threw down the dagger and went out. Tiberius, he said, was perfectly aware of what had happened, yet never dared question him or take any action in the matter.

Gaius' accession seemed to the Roman

people – one might almost say to the whole world – like the answer to their prayers. The memory of Germanicus and compassion for a family that had been practically wiped out by successive murders made most provincials and soldiers, many of whom had known him as a child, and the entire population of Rome as well, show extravagant joy that he was now emperor. When he escorted Tiberius' funeral procession from Misenum to Rome he was, of course, dressed in mourning, but a dense crowd greeted him ecstatically with altars, sacrifices and torches, and such endearments as 'star', 'chick', 'baby' and 'pet'.

On his arrival in the city the Senate (and a mob of people who had forced their way into the Senate House) immediately and unanimously conferred absolute power upon him. They set aside Tiberius' will, which made his other grandson, then still a child, joint heir with Gaius, and so splendid were the celebrations that 160,000 victims were publicly sacrificed during the next three months, or perhaps even a shorter period. A few days later he visited the prison islands off Campania, and vows were uttered for his safe return – at that time no opportunity of demonstrating a general concern for his welfare was ever disregarded. When he fell ill, anxious crowds besieged the Palatine all night. Some swore that they would fight as gladiators if the gods allowed him to recover; others even carried placards volunteering to die instead of him. To the great love in which he was held by his own people, foreigners added their own tribute of devotion. Artabanus, the king of the Parthians, who had always loathed and despised Tiberius, made unsolicited overtures of friendship to Gaius, attended a conference with the governor of Syria, and, before returning across the river Euphrates, paid homage to the Roman Eagles and standards and the statues of the Caesars.

Gaius strengthened his popularity by every possible means. He delivered a funeral speech in honour of Tiberius to a vast crowd, weeping profusely all the while, and gave him a magnificent burial. But as soon as this was over he sailed for Pandataria and the Pontian Islands to fetch back the remains of his mother and his brother Nero – and during rough weather too, in proof of devotion. He approached the ashes with the utmost reverence, and transferred them to the urns with his own hands. Equally dramatic was his gesture of raising a standard on the poop of the bireme which brought the urns to Ostia, and thence up the Tiber to Rome. He had arranged that the most distinguished *equites* available should carry them to the Mausoleum about noon, when the streets were at their busiest, and also appointed an annual day for commemorative rites, marked by chariot races in the Circus, at which Agrippina's image would be paraded in a covered carriage. He honoured his father's memory by renaming the month of September 'Germanicus', and sponsored a senatorial decree which awarded his grandmother Antonia, at a blow, all the honours won by Livia Augusta in her entire lifetime. As fellow consul he chose his uncle Claudius, who had hitherto been a mere *eques*, and adopted young Tiberius when he came of age, giving him the title of Youth Leader. He included the names of his sisters in the official oath which everyone had to take, which ran, 'I will not value my life or that of my children less highly than I do the safety of Gaius and his sisters,' and in the consular motions, as follows: 'Good fortune attend Gaius Caesar and his sisters!'

A similar bid for popularity was to recall all exiles and dismiss all criminal charges whatsoever that had been pending since the time of Tiberius. The batches of written evidence in his mother's and brothers' cases were brought to the Forum at his orders and burned, to set at rest the minds of such witnesses and informers as had testified against them, but first he swore before heaven that he had neither read nor abstracted a single document. He also refused to examine a report supposedly concerning his own safety, on the ground that nobody could have any reason to hate him, and swore that he would never listen to informers.

Gaius drove the spintrian perverts from the city, and could only with difficulty be restrained from drowning the lot. He gave permission for the works of Titus Labienus, Cremutius Cordus and Cassius Severus, which had been banned by order of the Senate, to be sought out and republished – making his desire known that posterity should be in full possession of all historical facts. In addition, he revived Augustus' practice, discontinued by Tiberius, of publishing an imperial budget, and invested the magistrates with full authority over court cases, not allowing litigants to come to him to appeal their decisions. He scrupulously scanned the list of *equites*, but, though publicly dismounting any who had behaved in a wicked or scandalous manner, was not unduly severe with those guilty of lesser misbehaviour – he merely omitted their names from the list which he read out. His creation of a fifth judicial division aided jurors to keep abreast of their work; his reviving of the electoral system was designed to restore voting rights to the people. He honoured every one of the bequests in Tiberius' will, though this had been set aside by the Senate, and in that of Julia Augusta, which Tiberius had suppressed; he abolished the Italian half-per-cent auction tax; and he paid compensation to a great many people whose houses had been damaged by fire. Any king whom he restored to the throne was awarded the taxes that had accumulated since his deposition – Antiochus of Commagene, for example, got a refund of 100 million sesterces. To show his interest in public morality, he awarded 800,000 sesterces to a freedwoman who, though put to extreme torture, had not revealed her patron's guilt. These acts won him many official honours, among them a golden shield, carried once a year to the Capitol by the colleges of priests marching in procession and followed by the Senate, while the children of the aristocracy chanted an anthem in praise of his virtues. By a senatorial decree, the day of his accession was called the Parilia, as though Rome had now been born again.

Gaius held four consulships: the earliest for two months, from the Kalends of July; the next for the whole month of January; the third for the first thirteen days of January; and the fourth for the first seven. Only the last two were in sequence. He assumed his third consulship at Lugdunum, without a colleague – not, as some people think, through arrogance or indifference, but because the news that his fellow consul-elect had died in Rome just before the Kalends of January had not reached him in time. He twice presented every member of the people with 300 sesterces, and twice invited all the senators and *equites*, with their wives and children, to an extravagant banquet. At the second of these banquets he gave every man a toga and every woman a purple scarf. In order to increase the public rejoicing in Rome for all time, he extended the Saturnalia with an additional day, which he called 'Youth Day'.

He held several gladiatorial contests, some in Statilius Taurus' amphitheatre and others in the Saepta, diversifying them with prize fights between the best boxers of Africa and Campania; he occasionally allowed magistrates or friends to preside at these instead of doing so himself. Again, he staged a great number of different theatrical shows in various buildings – sometimes at night, with the whole city illuminated – and would scatter vouchers among the audience entitling them to all sorts of gifts, over and above the basket of food which was everyone's due. At one banquet, noticing with what extraordinary gusto an *eques* seated opposite dug into the food, he sent him his own heaped plate as well, and rewarded a senator, who had been similarly enjoying himself, with a praetorship, though he was not yet qualified to hold this office. Many all-day games were celebrated in the Circus, and between races he introduced panther-baiting and the Troy Game. For certain special games, when all the charioteers were men of senatorial rank, he had the Circus decorated in red and green. Once, while he was inspecting the Circus equipment, from the Gelotian House which overlooks it, a group of people standing in the nearby balconies called out, 'What about a day's racing, Caesar?' So on the spur of the moment he gave immediate orders for games to be held.

One of his spectacles was on such a fantastic scale that nothing like it had ever been seen before. He collected all available merchant ships and anchored them in two lines, close together, the whole way from Baiae to the mole at Puteoli, a distance of three miles and some 600 feet. Then he had the ships boarded over, with earth heaped on the planks, and made a kind of Via Appia along which he trotted back and forth for two consecutive days. On the first day he wore a civic crown, a sword, a shield and a cloth-of-gold cloak, and rode a gaily caparisoned charger. On the second he appeared in charioteer's costume driving a team of two famous horses, with a boy named Dareus, one of his Parthian hostages, triumphantly displayed in the car beside him; behind came a force of praetorians and a group of his friends mounted in Gallic chariots. Gaius is of course generally supposed to have built the bridge as an improvement on Xerxes' famous feat of bridging the much narrower Helles-pont. Others believe that he planned this huge engineering feat to terrify the Germans and Britons, on whom he had his eye. But my grandfather used to tell me as a boy that, according to some courtiers in Gaius' confidence, the sole reason for the bridge was this: when Tiberius could not decide whom to appoint as his successor and inclined towards his grandson and namesake, Thrasyllus the astrologer had told him, 'As for Gaius, he has no more chance of becoming emperor than of riding a horse dry-shod across the Gulf of Baiae.'

Gaius gave several shows abroad – theatrical performances at Syracuse and mixed games at Lugdunum, where he also held a competition in Greek and Latin oratory. The losers, they say, had to present the winners with prizes and make speeches praising them, while those who failed miserably were forced to erase their entries with either sponges or their own tongues – at the threat of being thrashed and flung into the Rhône.

He completed certain projects neglected by Tiberius, namely the Temple of Augustus and Pompey's Theatre, and began the construction of an aqueduct in the Tibur district and an amphitheatre near the Saepta. (His successor Claudius finished the aqueduct, but work on the amphitheatre was abandoned.) Gaius rebuilt the ruinous walls and temples of Syracuse, and among his other projects were the restoration of Polycrates' palace at Samos, the completion of Didymaean Apollo's temple at Miletus, and the building of a city high up in the Alps. But he was most deeply interested in cutting a canal through the Isthmus of Corinth, and sent a *primipilaris* there to survey the site.

So much for Gaius the Emperor; the rest of this history must needs deal with Gaius the Monster.

He adopted a variety of titles, such as Pious, Son of the Camp, Father of the Army, Caesar Optimus Maximus. But when once, at the dinner table, some foreign kings who had come to pay homage were arguing which of them was the most nobly descended, he burst out, 'Nay, let there be one master, and one king!' And he nearly assumed a royal diadem then and there, transforming an ostensible principate into an actual kingdom. However, after his courtiers reminded him that he already outranked any king or local ruler, he insisted on being treated as a god – arranging for the most revered or artistically famous statues of the gods, including that of Jupiter at Olympia, to be brought from Greece and have their heads replaced by his own.

Next he extended his Palatine residence as far as the Forum, converted the shrine of Castor and Pollux into a vestibule, and would often stand between these divine brothers to be worshipped by all visitants, some of whom addressed him as 'Jupiter Latiaris'. He established a shrine to his own godhead, with priests, the costliest possible victims, and a life-sized golden image, which was dressed every day in clothes identical with those that he happened to be wearing. All the richest citizens tried to gain priesthoods here, either by influence or by bribery. Flamingos, peacocks, black grouse, guinea hens and pheasants were offered as sacrifices, each on a particular day. When the moon shone full and bright he always invited the moon goddess to his bed, and during the day he would indulge in whispered conversations with Jupiter Capitolinus, pressing his ear to the god's mouth and sometimes raising his voice in anger. Once he was overheard threatening the god, 'Either you throw me or I will throw you!' Finally he announced that Jupiter had persuaded him to share his home, and therefore connected the Palatine with the Capitol by throwing a bridge across the Temple of Divus Augustus; he next began building a new house inside the precincts of the Capitol itself, in order to live even nearer.

Because of Agrippa's humble origin Gaius loathed being described as his grandson, and would fly into a rage if anyone mentioned him, in speech or song, as an ancestor of the Caesars. He nursed a fantasy that his mother had been born of an incestuous union between Augustus and Julia, and, not content with thus discrediting Augustus' name, cancelled the annual commemorations of his victories at Actium and Sicily, declaring that they had proved the ruin of the Roman people. He called his great-grandmother Livia Augusta a 'Ulysses in petticoats', and in a letter to the Senate he dared describe her as of low birth – 'her maternal grandfather Aufidius Lurco having been a mere town councillor from Fundi' – although the public records showed Lurco to have held high office at Rome. When his paternal grand-mother Antonia begged him to grant her a private audience he insisted on taking Macro, the praetorian prefect, as his escort. Unkind treatment of this sort hurried her to the grave, though according to some he accelerated the process with poison; and when she died he showed so little respect that he sat in his din-ing room and watched the funeral pyre burn. He sent a military tribune to kill young Tiberius without warning, on the pretext that Tiberius had insulted him by taking an antidote against poison – his breath smelled of it – and he forced his father-in-law, Marcus Silanus, to cut his own throat with a razor, the charge being that he had not followed him when he put to sea in a storm, but had stayed on shore to seize power at Rome if anything happened to him. The truth was that Silanus, a notoriously bad sailor, could not face the voyage; and young Tiberius' breath smelled of medicine taken for a persistent cough which was gaining a hold on his lungs. Gaius preserved his uncle Claudius mainly as a butt for practical jokes.

It was his habit to commit incest with each of his three sisters in turn, and at large banquets, when his wife reclined above him, placed them all in turn below him. They say that he ravished his sister Drusilla before he came of age: their grandmother Antonia, at whose house they were both staying, caught them in bed together. Later, he took Drusilla from her husband, the former consul Lucius Cassius Longinus, quite unashamedly treating her as his wife; when he fell dangerously ill, he left her all his property, and the empire too. At her death he made it a capital offence to laugh, to bathe, or to dine with one's parents, wives or children while the period of public mourning lasted, and he was so crazed with grief that he suddenly rushed from Rome by night, drove through Campania, took ship to Sicily, and returned just as impetuously, without having shaved or cut his hair in the meantime. Afterwards, whenever he had to take an important oath, he swore by Drusilla's godhead, even at a public assembly or an army parade. He showed no such extreme love or respect for the two surviving sisters, and often, indeed, let his toy boys sleep with them; and at Aemilius Lepidus' trial he felt no compunction about denouncing them as adulteresses who were party to plots against him – openly producing letters in their handwriting (acquired by trickery and seduction) and dedicating to Mars Ultor the three swords with which, the accompanying placard alleged, they had meant to kill him.

It would be hard to say whether the way he got married, the way he dissolved his marriages or the way he behaved as a husband was the most disgraceful. He attended the wedding ceremony of Gaius Piso and Livia Orestilla, but had the bride carried off to his own home. After a few days, however, he sent her away, and two years later he banished her, suspecting that she had returned to Piso in the interval. According to one account, he told Piso, who was reclining opposite him at the wedding feast, 'Hands off my wife!' and took her home with him at once, and announced the next day that he had taken a wife in the style of Romulus and Augustus. Then he suddenly sent to the provinces for Lollia Paulina, wife of Gaius Memmius, the consular army commander, because somebody had remarked that her grandmother was once a famous beauty; but he soon discarded her, forbidding her ever again to sleep with another man. Caesonia was neither young nor beautiful and had three daughters by a former husband, besides being recklessly extravagant and utterly promiscuous, yet he loved her with a passionate faithfulness and often, when reviewing the troops, used to take her out riding in helmet, cloak and shield. For his friends he even paraded her naked, but he would not allow her the dignified title of wife until she had borne him a child, whereupon he announced the marriage and the birth simultaneously. He named the child Julia Drusilla, and carried her around the temples of all the goddesses in turn before finally entrusting her to the lap of Minerva, whom he called upon to supervise his daughter's growth and education. What he regarded as the surest proof of his paternity was her violent temper: while still an infant, she would try to scratch out her little playmates' eyes.

It seems hardly worthwhile to record how Gaius treated such relatives and friends as his cousin King Ptolemy (son of Juba and Mark Antony's daughter Selene) and even Macro and his wife Ennia, by whose help he had become emperor. Their very loyalty and nearness to him earned them cruel deaths. Nor was he any more respectful or considerate in his dealings with the Senate, but made some of the highest officials run for miles beside his chariot, dressed in their togas, or wait in short linen tunics at the head or foot of his dining couch. Often he would send for men whom he had secretly killed, as though they were still alive, and remark offhandedly a few days later that they must have committed suicide. When the consuls forgot to announce his birthday, he dismissed them and left the commonwealth for three days without its chief officers. One of his quaestors was charged

with conspiracy; Gaius had his clothes stripped off
and spread on the ground, to give the soldiers who
flogged him a firmer foothold.

He behaved just as arrogantly and violently towards
people of less exalted rank. A crowd bursting into
the Circus in the middle of the night to secure free
seats angered him so much that he had them driven
away with clubs; more than a score of *equites*, as many
married women, and numerous others were crushed
to death in the ensuing panic. Gaius liked to stir up
trouble in the theatre by scattering gift vouchers
before the seats were occupied, thus tempting the
common people to invade the rows reserved for
equites. During gladiatorial shows he would have the
canopies removed at the hottest time of the day and
forbid anyone to leave; or cancel the regular pro-
gramme and substitute worn-out wild beasts and
feeble old fighters; or stage comic duels between
respectable householders who happened to be physically disabled in some way or other. More than once
he closed down the granaries and let the people go
hungry.

The following instances will illustrate his cruelty.
Having collected wild animals for one of his shows,

he found butcher's meat too expensive and decided to feed them with criminals instead. He paid no attention to the charge sheets, but simply stood in the middle of a colonnade, glanced at the prisoners lined up before him, and gave the order 'Kill every man between that bald head and that other one over there.' Someone had sworn to fight in the arena if he recovered from his illness; Gaius forced him to fulfil this oath and watched his swordplay closely, not letting him go until he had won the match and begged abjectly to be released. Another fellow had pledged himself on the same occasion to commit suicide; Gaius, finding that he was still alive, ordered him to be dressed in wreaths and fillets and driven through Rome by the imperial slaves, who kept harping on his pledge and finally flung him over the rampart. Many men of decent family were branded at his command and sent down the mines, or put to work on the roads, or thrown to the wild beasts. Others were confined in narrow cages, where they had to crouch on all fours like animals, or were sawn in half – and not necessarily for major offences, but merely for criticizing his shows, failing to swear by his *genius*, and so forth.

Gaius made parents attend their sons' executions, and when one father excused himself on the ground of ill health he provided a litter for him. Having invited another father to dinner just after the son's execution, he overflowed with good fellowship in an attempt to make him laugh and joke. He watched the manager of his gladiatorial and wild-beast shows being flogged with chains for several days running, and had him killed only when the smell of suppurating brains became insupportable. A writer of Atellan farces was burned alive in the amphitheatre, because of a single line which had an amusing double entendre. One *eques*, on the point of being thrown to the wild beasts, shouted that he was innocent; Gaius brought him back, removed his tongue, and then ordered the sentence to be carried out.

Once he asked a returned exile how he had been spending his time. To flatter him the man answered, 'I prayed continuously to the gods for Tiberius' death and your accession, and my prayer was granted.' Gaius therefore concluded that the new batch of exiles must be praying for his own death, so he sent agents from island to island and had them all killed. Being anxious that one particular senator should be torn in pieces, he persuaded some of his colleagues to challenge him as a public enemy when he entered the Senate House, stab him with their pens, and then hand him over for lynching to the rest of the Senate; and he was not satisfied until the victim's limbs, organs and guts had been dragged through the streets and heaped up at his feet.

His savage crimes were matched by his brutal language. He claimed that no personal trait made him feel prouder than his 'inflexibility' – by which he must have meant 'brazen impudence'. As though mere deafness to his grandmother Antonia's good advice were not enough, he told her, 'Bear in mind that I can do anything I want to anyone I want!' Suspecting that young Tiberius had taken drugs as prophylactics to the poison he intended to administer, Gaius scoffed, 'Can there really be an antidote against Caesar?' And on banishing his sisters he remarked, 'I have swords as well as islands.' One man of praetorian status, taking a cure at Anticyra, made frequent requests for an extension of his sick leave; Gaius had his throat cut, suggesting that if hellebore had been of so little benefit over so long a period, he must need to be bled. When signing the execution list after the ten-day waiting period he used to say, 'I am clearing my accounts.' And one day, after sentencing a number of Gauls and Greeks to die in the same batch, he boasted of having 'subdued Gallograecia'.

The method of execution he preferred was to inflict numerous small wounds, avoiding the prisoner's vital organs, and his familiar order 'Make him feel that he is dying!' soon became proverbial. Once, when the wrong man had been killed, owing to a confusion of names, he announced that the victim had equally deserved death, and he often quoted the tragic line 'Let them hate me, so long as they fear me.' He would indiscriminately abuse the Senate as having been supporters of Sejanus or informers against his mother and brothers (at this point producing the papers which he was supposed to have burned), and exclaim that Tiberius' cruelty had been quite justified since, with so many accusers about, he was bound to believe their charges. The *equites* earned his constant displeasure for spending their time, or so he complained, at the plays or the games. On one occasion the people cheered the wrong team; he cried angrily, 'I wish all you Romans had only one neck!' When a shout arose in the amphitheatre for Tetrinius the bandit to come out and fight, he said that all those who called for him were Tetriniuses too. A group of net-and-trident gladiators, dressed in tunics, put up a very poor show against the five men-at-arms with whom they were matched; but when he sentenced them to death for cowardice, one of them seized a trident and killed each of his opponents in turn. Gaius then publicly expressed his horror at what he called 'this most bloody murder', and his disgust with those who had been able to stomach the sight.

He went about complaining how bad the times were, and particularly that there had been no public disasters like the Varus massacre under Augustus or the collapse of the amphitheatre at Fidenae under Tiberius. The prosperity of his own reign, he said, would lead to its being wholly forgotten, and he often prayed for a great military catastrophe or for famine, plague, fire or at least an earthquake.

Everything that Gaius said and did was marked with equal cruelty, even during his hours of rest and amusement and banquetry. He frequently had trials by torture held in his presence while he was eating or otherwise enjoying himself, and kept an expert headsman in readiness to decapitate the prisoners brought in from jail. When the bridge across the sea at Puteoli was being dedicated, he invited a number of spectators from the shore to inspect it and then abruptly tipped them into the water; some clung to the ships' rudders, but he had them dislodged with boathooks and oars and left to drown. At a public dinner in Rome he sent to his executioners a slave who had stolen a strip of silver from a couch; they were to lop off the man's hands, tie them around his neck so that they hung on his breast, and take him for a tour of the tables, displaying a placard in explanation of his punishment. On another occasion a gladiator against whom he was fencing with a wooden sword fell down deliberately, whereupon Gaius drew a real dagger, stabbed him to death, and ran about waving the palm branch of victory. Once, while serving at an altar in the role of sacrificial assistant, he swung his mallet as if at the victim, but instead felled his fellow assistant, whose duty it was to slit its throat. At one particularly extravagant banquet he burst into sudden peals of laughter. The consuls, who were reclining next to him, politely asked whether they might share the joke. 'What do you think?' he answered. 'It occurred to me that I have only to give one nod and both your throats will be cut on the spot!'

He played a prank on Apelles, the tragic actor, by striking a pose beside a statue of Jupiter and asking, 'Which of us two is the greater?' When Apelles hesitated momentarily, Gaius had him flogged, commenting on the musical quality even of his groans for mercy. He never kissed the neck of his wife or mistress without saying, 'And this beautiful throat will be cut whenever I please.' Sometimes he even threatened to torture Caesonia as a means of discovering why he was so devoted to her.

In his insolent pride and destructiveness he made malicious attacks on men of almost every epoch. Needing more room in the Capitol courtyard, Augustus had once shifted the statues of certain famous men to the Campus Martius; these Gaius dashed to the ground and shattered so completely that they could not possibly be restored, even though their bases were intact. After this no statue or bust of any living person could be set up without his permission. He toyed with the idea of suppressing Homer's poems – for surely, he would say, he might claim

35

Plato's privilege of banishing Homer from his republic. As for Virgil and Livy, Gaius came very near to having their works and busts removed from the libraries, claiming that Virgil had little knowledge and less skill and that Livy was a wordy and inaccurate historian. It seems also that he proposed to abolish the study of law; at any rate, he often swore by Hercules that no legal expert's advice would ever thwart his will.

Gaius deprived the noblest men at Rome of their ancient family emblems – Torquatus lost his golden torc, Cincinnatus his lock of hair, and Gnaeus Pompeius the famous cognomen Magnus. He invited King Ptolemy to visit Rome, welcomed him with appropriate honours, and then suddenly ordered his execution – as mentioned above – because at Ptolemy's entrance into the amphitheatre during a gladiatorial show the fine purple cloak which he wore had attracted universal admiration. Any good-looking man with a fine head of hair whom Gaius ran across had the back of his scalp brutally shaved. One Aesius Proculus, the son of a *primipilaris*, was so well built and handsome that people nicknamed him 'Colosseros'. Without warning, Gaius ordered Aesius to be dragged from his seat in the amphitheatre into the arena and matched first with a Thracian net fighter, then with a man-at-arms. Though Aesius won both combats, he was thereupon dressed in rags, led fettered through the streets to be jeered at by women, and finally strangled. In short, however low anyone's fortune or condition might be, Gaius always found some cause for envy. Thus he sent a stronger man to challenge the current King of the Grove, simply because he had held his priesthood for a number of years. A chariot fighter called Porius drew such tremendous applause for freeing his slave in celebration of a victory at the games that Gaius indignantly rushed from the amphitheatre. In so doing he tripped over the fringe of his robe and pitched down the steps, at the bottom of which he complained that the most powerful race in the world seemed to take greater notice of a gladiator's trifling gesture than of all their deified emperors, even the one still among them.

He had not the slightest regard for chastity, either his own or others', and is said to have had sexual relations, both active and passive, with Marcus Lepidus, Mnester the pantomime dancer, and various foreign hostages; moreover, a young man of consular family, Valerius Catullus, publicly announced that Gaius had been his passive sexual partner and had completely exhausted him with his demands. Besides incest with his sisters, and a notorious passion for the prostitute Pyrallis, Gaius made advances to almost every well-known married woman in Rome; after inviting a selection of them to dinner with their husbands, he would slowly and carefully examine each in turn while they passed his couch, as a purchaser might assess the value of a slave, and even stretch out his hand and lift up the chin of any woman who kept her eyes modestly cast down. Then, whenever he felt so inclined, he would send for whoever pleased him best and leave the banquet in her company. A little later he would return, showing obvious signs of what he had been about, and openly discuss his bedfellow in detail, dwelling on her good and bad physical points and criticizing her sexual performance. To some of these unfortunates he issued, and publicly registered, divorces in the name of their absent husbands.

No parallel can be found for Gaius' far-fetched extravagances. He invented new kinds of baths and the most unnatural dishes and drinks – bathing in hot and cold perfumes, drinking valuable pearls dissolved in vinegar, and providing his guests with golden bread and golden meat; he would remark that Caesar alone could not afford to be frugal. For several days in succession he scattered large sums of money from the roof of the Basilica Julia, and he built Liburnian galleys with ten banks of oars, jewelled poop decks, multicoloured sails, and huge baths, colonnades and banqueting halls aboard – not to mention growing vines and fruit trees of different varieties. In these vessels he used to take day-long cruises along the Campanian coast, reclining on his couch and listening to songs and choruses. Villas and country houses were run up for him regardless of expense. In fact Gaius seemed interested only in doing the apparently impossible, which led him to construct moles in deep, rough water far out to sea, drive tunnels through exceptionally hard rocks, raise flat ground to the height of mountains, and reduce mountains to the level of plains – and all at immense speed, because he punished delay with death. But why give details? Suffice it to record that in less than a year he squandered Tiberius' entire fortune of 2,700 million sesterces, and an enormous amount of other treasure besides.

When bankrupt and in need of funds, Gaius concentrated on wickedly ingenious methods of raising funds by false accusations, auctions, and taxes. He ruled that no man could inherit the Roman citizenship acquired by any ancestor more remote than his father, and when confronted with certificates of citizenship issued by Divus Julius or Divus Augustus he rejected them as obsolete. He also disallowed all property returns to which, for whatever reason, later additions had been appended. If a *primipilaris* had bequeathed nothing either to Tiberius or himself since the beginning of the former's reign, he would rescind the will on the ground of ingratitude, and he likewise voided the wills of all other persons who were said to have intended making him their heir when they died but had not done so. This caused widespread alarm, so that people would openly declare that he was one of their heirs, with strangers listing him among their friends and parents among their children; but if they continued to live after the declaration he considered himself tricked, and sent several of them presents of poisoned sweets. Gaius conducted these cases in person, first announcing the sum he meant to raise, and not stopping until he had raised it. The slightest delay nettled him; he once passed a single sentence on a batch of more than forty men charged with various offences, and then boasted to Caesonia, when she woke from her nap, that he had done very good business since she dozed off.

He would auction whatever properties were left over from a theatrical show, driving up the bidding to such heights that many of those present, forced to buy at fantastic prices, found themselves ruined and committed suicide by opening their veins. A famous occasion was when Aponius Saturninus fell asleep on a bench, and Gaius warned the auctioneer to keep an eye on the senator of praetorian rank who kept nodding his head. Before the bidding ended Aponius had unwittingly bought thirteen gladiators for a total of 9 million sesterces.

While in Gaul, Gaius did so well by selling the furniture, jewellery, slaves and even the freedmen of his condemned sisters at a ridiculous overvaluation that he decided to do the same with the furnishings of the old palace. So he sent to Rome, where his agents commandeered public conveyances and even draught animals from the bakeries to fetch the stuff north; this led to a bread shortage in Rome and to the loss of many lawsuits, because litigants who lived at a distance were unable to appear in court and meet their bail. He then used all kinds of tricks for disposing of the furniture: scolding the bidders for their avarice or for their shamelessness in being richer than he was, and pretending grief at this surrender of family property to commoners. Discovering that one wealthy provincial had paid his stewards 200,000 sesterces to be smuggled into a banquet, Caligula was delighted that the privilege of dining with him should be valued so highly, and when next day the same man turned up at the auction he made him pay 200,000 sesterces for some trifling object – but also sent him a personal invitation to dinner.

The publicans were ordered to raise new and unprecedented taxes, and found this so profitable that he detailed the tribunes and centurions of the praetorian guards to collect the money instead. No goods or services now avoided duty of some kind. He imposed a fixed tax on all foodstuffs sold in any quarter of the city, and a charge of 2½ per cent on the money involved in every lawsuit and legal transaction whatsoever, and also devised special penalties for anyone who settled out of court or abandoned a case. Porters had to hand over an eighth part of their day's earnings, and prostitutes their standard fee for a single act of intimacy, even if they had quitted their profession and were respectably married; pimps and ex-pimps also became liable to this public tax.

These new regulations having been announced by word of mouth only, many people failed to observe them through ignorance. At last he acceded to the urgent popular demand by posting the regulations up, but in an awkwardly cramped spot and written so small that no one could take a copy. He never missed a chance of making profits: setting aside a suite of rooms on the Palatine, he decorated them worthily, opened a brothel, stocked it with married women and freeborn boys, and then sent his pages around the squares and public places, inviting men of all ages to come and enjoy themselves. Those who appeared were lent money at interest, and clerks wrote down their names under the heading 'Contributors to Caesar's Revenue'.

Even when Gaius played at dice he would always

cheat and lie. Once he interrupted a game by giving up his seat to the man behind him and going out into the courtyard. A couple of rich *equites* passed; he immediately had them arrested and confiscated their property, and then resumed the game in high spirits, boasting that his luck had never been better.

His daughter's birth gave him an excuse for further complaints of poverty. 'In addition to the burden of sovereignty,' he said, 'I must now shoulder that of fatherhood' – and he promptly took up a collection for her education and dowry. He also announced that good-luck gifts would be welcomed on the Kalends of January, and then sat in the palace porch, grabbing the handfuls and capfuls of coins which a mixed crowd of all classes pressed on him. At last he developed a passion for the feel of money and, spilling heaps of gold pieces on an open space, would walk over them barefoot or else lie down and wallow.

Gaius had only a single taste of warfare, and even that was unpremeditated. At Mevania, where he went to visit the river Clitumnus and its sacred grove, he was reminded that he needed Batavian recruits for his bodyguard, and this suggested the idea of a

German expedition. He wasted no time in summoning legions and auxiliaries from all directions, levied troops with the utmost strictness, and collected military supplies on an unprecedented scale. Then he marched off with such rapidity that the praetorian cohorts could not keep up with him except by breaking tradition and tying their standards on the pack mules. Yet later he became so lazy and self-indulgent that he travelled in a litter borne by eight bearers, and whenever he approached a town he made the inhabitants sweep the roads and lay the dust with sprinklers.

After reaching the camp, Gaius showed how keen and severe a commander he intended to be by ignominiously dismissing any legate who was late in bringing along the auxiliaries he required. Then, when he reviewed the legions, he discharged several veteran *primipilares* on grounds of age and incapacity, though some had only a few more days of their service to run, and, calling the remainder a pack of greedy fellows, scaled down their retirement bonus to 6,000 sesterces each.

All that he accomplished in this expedition was to receive the surrender of Adminius, son of the British king Cynobellinus, who had been banished by his father and come over to the Romans with a few followers. Gaius nevertheless wrote an extravagant dispatch which might have persuaded any reader that the whole island had surrendered to him, and ordered the couriers to drive their chariots all the way to the Forum and the Senate House and to deliver his letter to the consuls in the Temple of Mars in the presence of the entire Senate.

Since the chance of military action appeared very remote, he soon ordered a few German prisoners to be taken across the Rhine and hidden among the trees. After lunch, scouts hurried in to tell him excitedly that the enemy were upon him. He at once galloped out at the head of his staff and part of the praetorian cavalry to halt in the nearest thicket, where they chopped branches from the trees and dressed them like trophies; then, riding back by torchlight, he taunted as cowards all who had failed to follow him and awarded his fellow heroes a novel fashion in crowns – he called it 'The Ranger's Crown' – ornamented with sun, moon and stars. On another day he took some German hostages from a school where they were being taught the rudiments of Latin and secretly ordered them on ahead of him. Later he left his dinner in a hurry and took his cavalry in pursuit of them, as though they had been fugitives. He was no less melodramatic about this foray: when he returned to the hall after catching the hostages and bringing them back in irons, and his officers reported that the army was marshalled, he made them recline at table, still in their corselets, and quoted Virgil's famous advice: 'Be steadfast, comrades, and preserve yourselves for happier occasions.' He also severely reprimanded the absent Senate and People for enjoying banquets and festivities and for hanging about the theatres or their luxurious country houses while their Caesar was exposed to all the hazards of war.

In the end, he drew up his army in battle array on the shore of the Ocean and moved the siege engines into position as though he intended to bring the campaign to a close. No one had the least notion what was in his mind, when suddenly he gave the order 'Gather seashells!' He referred to the shells as 'plunder from the sea, due to the Capitol and to the Palatine', and made the troops fill their helmets and the folds of their clothes with them; he commemorated this victory by the erection of a tall lighthouse, not unlike the one at Pharos, in which fires were to be kept going all night as a guide to ships. Then he promised every soldier a bounty of 100 denarii, and told them, 'Go rich, go happy!', as though he had surpassed every standard of generosity.

He now concentrated his attention on the imminent triumph. To supplement the few prisoners taken in frontier skirmishes and the deserters who had come over from the barbarians, he picked the tallest Gauls of the province – 'those worthy of a triumph', as he himself said – and some of their leaders as well, for his supposed train of captives. These had not only to grow their hair and dye it red, but also to learn Germanic speech and adopt Germanic names. The triremes used in the Ocean were carted to Rome, overland for most of the way. He sent a letter ahead instructing his agents to prepare a triumph more lavish than any hitherto known, but at the least possible expense, and added that everyone's property was at their disposal.

Before leaving Gaul he planned, in a sudden access of cruelty, to massacre the legionaries who, at news of Augustus' death, had mutinously besieged both his father Germanicus, their commander, and himself, still only a baby. His friends barely restrained him from carrying out this plan, and could not at all dissuade him from deciding on a decimation. And so he summoned the troops to assemble without any arms, even their swords, and surrounded them with armed horsemen. But when he noticed that a number of legionaries, scenting trouble, were slipping away to fetch their weapons, he hurriedly absconded and headed straight for Rome. There, to distract attention from his inglorious exploits, he vengefully threatened the Senate, who he said had cheated him of a well-earned triumph – though in point of fact he had expressly stated a few days before that they must do nothing to honour him, on pain of death.

So, when the distinguished senatorial delegates met him with an official plea for his immediate return, he shouted, 'I am coming, never fear, and this' – tapping the hilt of his sword – 'is coming too!' He proclaimed that he was returning only to those who would really welcome him, namely the *equites* and the people; so far as the senators were concerned, he would never again consider himself their fellow citizen or their *princeps*, and he even forbade any more of them to meet him. Having cancelled or at least

49

postponed his triumph, he entered the city on his birthday and received an ovation. Within four months he was dead.

Gaius had dared commit fearful crimes and contemplated even worse ones, such as murdering the most distinguished of the senators and *equites* and then moving the seat of government first to Antium and afterwards to Alexandria. If at this point my readers become incredulous, let me record that two notebooks were found among his private papers entitled *Dagger* and *Sword*, each of them containing the names and particulars of men whom he had planned to kill. A huge chest filled with poisons also came to light. It is said that when Claudius later threw this into the sea, quantities of dead fish, cast up by the tide, littered the neighbouring beaches.

Gaius was tall, with a pallid complexion; he had a large body, but a thin neck and spindly legs; his eyes were sunken and his temples hollow, although his forehead was broad and forbidding. In contrast to his noticeably hairy body, the hair on his head was thin, and his crown was completely bald. Because of his baldness and hairiness, he announced that it was a capital offence for anyone either to look down on him as he passed or to mention goats in any context. He worked hard to make his naturally uncouth face even more repulsive by practising fearful grimaces in front of a mirror.

As to his health, Gaius was sick both physically and mentally. As a boy, he suffered from epilepsy, and, although his resistance to the disease gradually strengthened, there were times in his youth when he could hardly walk, stand, think or hold up his head, owing to sudden fits. He was well aware that he had mental trouble, and sometimes proposed taking a leave of absence from Rome to clear his brain; Caesonia is reputed to have given him an aphrodisiac which drove him mad. Insomnia was his worst torment. Three hours a night of fitful sleep were all that he ever got, and even then terrifying visions would haunt him – once, for instance, he dreamed that he had a conversation with the sea. He tired of lying awake the greater part of the night, and would alternately sit up in bed and wander through the long corridors, invoking the day which seemed as if it would never break.

I am convinced that this mental illness accounted for his two contradictory vices – overconfidence and extreme timorousness. Here was a man who despised the gods, yet shut his eyes and buried his head beneath the bedclothes at the most distant sound of thunder; and if the storm came closer he would jump out of bed and crawl underneath. In his travels through Sicily he poked fun at the miraculous stories associated with the various locales, yet on reaching Messana he suddenly fled in the middle of the night, terrified by the smoke and noise which came from the crater of Aetna. Despite his fearful threats against the barbarians, he showed so little courage after he had crossed the Rhine and gone riding in a chariot through a defile that when someone happened to remark 'What a panic there would be if the enemy unexpectedly appeared!' he leaped on a horse and galloped back to the bridges. These were crowded with army transport, but he had himself passed from hand to hand over the men's heads in his haste to regain the further bank. Even when safely home he was alarmed by reported revolts in Germany and decided to escape by sea. He fitted out a large fleet for this purpose, finding comfort only in the thought that, should the enemy be victorious and occupy the Alpine passes, as the Cimbri had done, or Rome, as the Senones had done, he would at least be able to hold his overseas provinces. This was probably what later gave his assassins the idea of quieting his vengeful German bodyguard with the story that rumours of a defeat had scared him into sudden suicide.

Gaius paid no attention to traditional or current fashions in his dress, but ignored masculine and even human conventions. Often he made public appearances in a cloak covered with embroidery and encrusted with precious stones, a long-sleeved tunic, and bracelets, and at other times in silk or even a woman's gown; and he came shod sometimes with slippers, sometimes with buskins, sometimes with military boots, sometimes with women's shoes. Occasionally he affected a golden beard and carried Jupiter's thunderbolt, Neptune's trident or Mercury's caduceus. He even dressed up as Venus, and long before his expedition he wore the uniform of a triumphant general, often embellished with the breastplate which he had stolen from the tomb of Alexander the Great.

Though no man of letters, Gaius took pains to study oratory, and showed remarkable eloquence and quickness of mind, especially when prosecuting.

Anger incited him to a flood of verbiage; he moved about excitedly while speaking, and his voice carried a great distance. At the start of every speech he would threaten to 'draw the sword which he had forged in his midnight study'; yet he so despised more elegant and melodious styles that he discounted Seneca, then at the height of his fame, as a 'mere textbook orator' and 'sand without lime'. He often published confutations of speakers who had successfully pleaded a case, or composed speeches for both the prosecution and the defence of important men who were on trial by the Senate – the verdict depending entirely on the caprice of his pen – and would invite the *equites* by proclamation to attend and listen.

Gaius practised many other arts – most enthusiastically too. He made appearances as a Thracian gladiator and a charioteer, as a singer and a dancer; he would fight with real weapons and drive chariots in the circuses that he had built in many places. Indeed, he was so proud of his singing and dancing that he could not resist the temptation of supporting the tragic actors at public performances, and would repeat their gestures by way of praise or criticism. On the very day of his death he seems to have ordered an all-night festival so that he could take advantage of the free-and-easy atmosphere to make his stage debut. He often danced even at night, and once, at the close of the second watch, summoned three senators of consular rank to the palace; arriving half-dead with fear, they were conducted to a stage upon which, amid a tremendous racket of flutes and castanets, Gaius suddenly burst, dressed in a shawl and an ankle-length tunic; he performed a song and dance, and disappeared as suddenly as he had entered. Yet with all these gifts he could not swim a stroke!

On those whom he loved he bestowed an almost insane passion. He would shower kisses on Mnester the pantomime dancer even in the theatre, and if anyone made the slightest noise during his performances Gaius had the offender dragged from his seat and beat him with his own hands. To an *eques* who created some disturbance while Mnester was on the stage, Gaius sent instructions by a centurion to sail from Ostia and convey a sealed message to King Ptolemy in Mauretania. The message read, 'Do nothing at all, either good or bad, to the bearer.'

He chose Thracian gladiators to officer his German bodyguard. Disliking the men-at-arms, he reduced their defensive armour; and when a gladiator of this sort, called Columbus, won a fight but was lightly wounded, Gaius treated him with a virulent poison which he afterwards called 'Columbinum' – at any rate that was how he described it in his catalogue of poisons. Gaius supported the Green faction with such ardour that he would often dine and spend the night in their stables, and on one occasion he gave the driver Eutychus presents worth 2 million sesterces. To prevent Incitatus, his favourite horse, from growing restive he always picketed the neighbourhood with troops on the day before the races, ordering them to enforce absolute silence. Incitatus owned a marble stable, an ivory stall, purple blankets and a jewelled collar, as well as a house, furniture and slaves – to provide suitable entertainment for guests whom Gaius invited in its name. It is said that he even planned to award Incitatus a consulship.

Such frantic and reckless behaviour roused murderous thoughts in certain minds. One or two plots for his assassination were discovered; others were still maturing when two tribunes of the praetorian guard put their heads together and succeeded in killing him, thanks to the cooperation of his most powerful freedmen and the praetorian prefects. Both these tribunes had been accused of being implicated in a previous plot and, although innocent, realized that Gaius hated and feared them. Once, in fact, he had subjected them to public shame and suspicion, taking them aside and announcing, as he waved a sword, that he would gladly kill himself if they thought him deserving of death. After this he accused them again and again, each to the other, and tried to make bad blood between them. At last they decided to kill him about noon at the conclusion of the Palatine Games, the principal part in this drama of blood being claimed by Cassius Chaerea. Gaius had persistently teased Cassius, who was no longer young, for his supposed effeminacy. Whenever he demanded the watchword, Gaius used to give him 'Priapus' or 'Venus'; and if he came to acknowledge a favour he always stuck out his middle finger for him to kiss, and wiggled it obscenely.

Many omens of Gaius' approaching death were reported. While the statue of Jupiter at Olympia was being dismantled before removal to Rome at his command, it burst into such a roar of laughter that the scaffolding collapsed and the workmen took to their heels, and a man named Cassius appeared immediately afterwards saying that Jupiter had ordered him in a dream to sacrifice a bull. The Capitol at Capua was struck by lightning on the Ides of March, which some interpreted as portending another death of the same sort that had previously occurred on that day. At Rome, the Palatine steward's lodge was likewise struck, and this seemed to mean that the master of the house stood in danger of attack by his own guards. On asking the astrologer Sulla for his horoscope, Gaius learned that he must expect to die very soon. The oracle of the goddesses of Fortune at Antium likewise warned him, 'Beware of Cassius!'; whereupon, forgetting Chaerea's nomen, he ordered the murder of Cassius Longinus, the consular governor of Asia. On the night before his assassination he dreamed that he was standing beside Jupiter's heavenly throne, when the god kicked him with the great toe of his right foot and sent him tumbling down to earth.